AUSCHWITZ

PASCAL CROCI

"And how long have you been keeping all this to yourself?"

"For fifty-two years! I'm telling you—before, no one was interested in any of that..."

— Maurice Minkowski, witness from Auschwitz-Birkenau

Harry N. Abrams, Inc., Publishers

AT THE DAWN OF CIVILIZATION, THE CHRISTIANS DECLARED: "IF YOU REMAIN JEWS, YOU SHALL NOT LIVE AMONGST US."
IN THE HIGH MIDDLE AGES, THE SECULAR LEADERS DECIDED: "YOU SHALL NO LONGER LIVE AMONGST US."
FINALLY, THE NAZIS DECREED: "YOU SHALL NO LONGER LIVE."

1993...
FORMER YUGOSLAVIA
KAZAL

WE HAVE NO RIGHT TO FORGET IT.
AUSCHWITZ HAS SHATTERED OUR LIVES.

KEEPING SILENT HAS KEPT US SANE.

A DELUSION, YOU MEAN.

THAT'S NOT TRUE!
SINCE OUR RETURN, WE'VE ONLY BEEN HALF LIVING.

WE HAVE BECOME THE LIVING DEAD!

CESSIA, ARE WE GOING TO DIE LIKE THIS TOO?

KAZIK, I BEG YOU, STOP!
THAT'S ENOUGH! THE TIME HAS COME TO OPEN UP THE CLOSETS.

THEY WERE SENDING US THERE TO WORK OUT IN THE FRESH AIR.

...
THAT'S WHAT YOUR MOTHER SAID.

REMEMBER!

WHEN THEY SAW THE TRAINS PASS, MOST OF THE POLES WOULD LAUGH, THEY WERE REJOICING...

THEY WERE GETTING RID OF THE JEWS!

IN FOUR DAYS, OUR WHOLE WORLD WAS TURNED UPSIDE DOWN.

MARCH 1944... THAT KID BESIDE THE TRACK, I CAN SEE HIM NOW!

RAUS !!!
RAUS SCHNELL!!
LEAVE YOUR LUGGAGE! MOVE ON TOWARD THE TRUCKS!
SCHNELL!
RAUS !!!
WHAT A STENCH! GET THOSE CARS EMPTIED OUT, AND MOVE IT!
WHERE ARE WE?
AUSCHWITZ
AUSCHWITZ?!
MA'AM!
Deutsche
!?
SHH, TRUST ME…
SAMUEL!

MY BABY!
WHATEVER YOU DO, DON'T MOVE!
HEY, YOU! WHERE ARE YOU GOING WITH THAT KID?
...
I ASKED YOU A QUESTION, ANSWER ME!
!?
GRANDMA, TAKE THIS CHILD WITH YOU!
NO!
SOLDIER! YOU HAVE NO IDEA HOW TO GET RESPECT...
THE ONLY WAY...
AAAVLAMH!
IS THIS!

UNDERSTAND?

THE REST OF YOU, GET BACK IN LINE!

AND MOVE IT!

WHY DID YOU MURDER THAT MAN?
?

WHAT WAS THE REASON?

WE ARE NOT CATTLE!

PICK THAT UP!!!
WHY SHOULD I?

OBEY, YOU JEWISH BITCH! HERE THERE ARE NO WHYS!

PICK THAT STAR UP BEFORE I COUNT TO THREE, OR YOU'VE HAD IT!

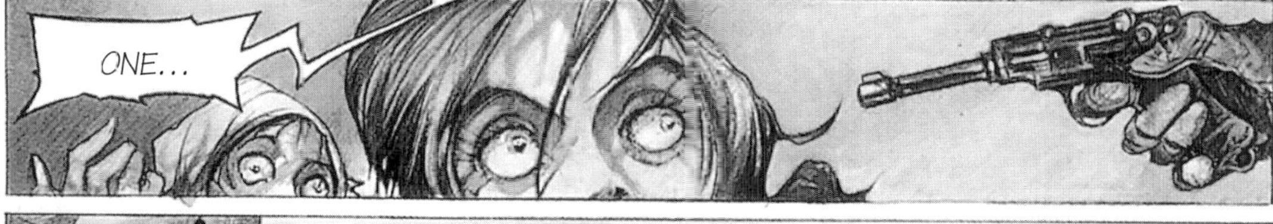
ONE...

TWO...

KEEP FACING THE OTHER WAY!

RUNNING THIS CAMP IS NOT A DELICATE AFFAIR!

!?

OBERSCHARFS-FÜHRER, DO YOU WANT TOTAL PANIC TO BREAK OUT?

WHY, DON'T YOU LIKE MY STYLE?
PUT AWAY THAT GUN. IT IS POSSIBLE TO CARRY OUT AN EFFICIENT SELECTION CALMLY.

RECHTS!
MEN TO THE RIGHT!
WOMEN TO THE LEFT!

WOMEN, LINE UP!

RIGHT!

LEFT!
YOU!

DON'T YOU UNDERSTAND WHAT I SAY?
...

BUT WHAT ARE YOU GOING TO DO WITH US?

WHY SEPARATE US?

IT'S JUST A ROUTINE FORMALITY, MA'AM! ALL FAMILIES WILL BE REUNITED AS SOON AS THE DISINFECTION IS COMPLETE.

VORWÄRTS SCHNELL!

THIS GROUP FOLLOW ME!

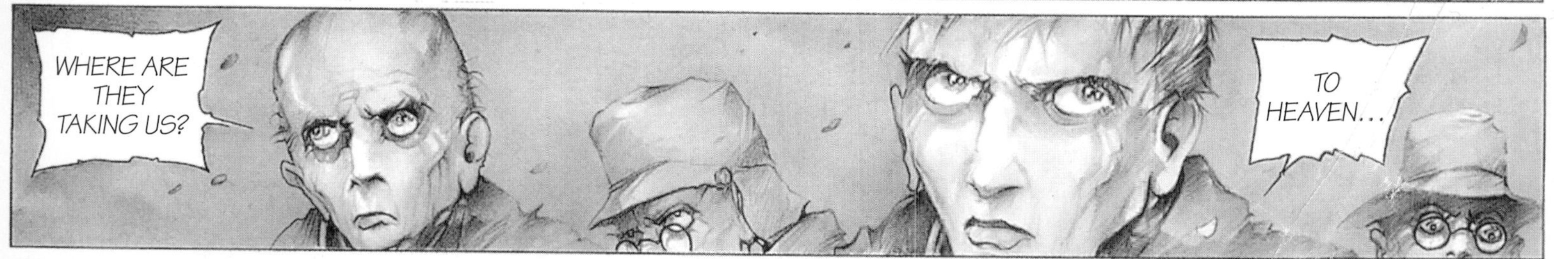
WHERE ARE THEY TAKING US?
TO HEAVEN...

WHAT?
CAN'T YOU SEE THE ANGELS?
SILENCE UP FRONT, KEEP MOVING!

GET UNDRESSED!

COMPLETELY, FROM TOP TO BOTTOM!!

IT ISN'T SNOW…IT'S ASH.

THEY'RE BURNING YOUR WIVES AND CHILDREN!

THEY'RE BURNING YOUR WIVES AND CHILDREN!

IN THIS PLACE, YOU COME IN THROUGH THE DOOR, AND YOU LEAVE THROUGH THE CHIMNEY….

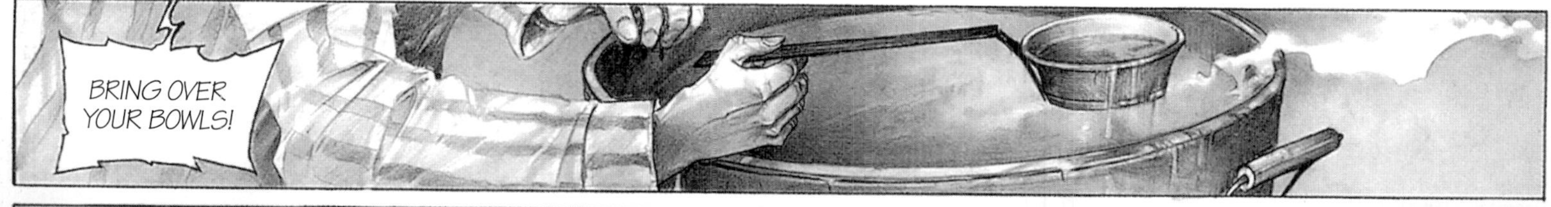
BRING OVER YOUR BOWLS!

SO THE NEW GUY'S MAKING FACES, EH?
...

HEY, LOST YOUR TONGUE?
OW!

GO ON, HURRY UP OR YOU'LL GET NOTHING TO EAT!

HEY, YOU! WAIT A MINUTE! REMEMBER—IN THIS PLACE, YOUR ONLY GUARDIAN ANGEL IS ME, GOT IT?

CHEW IT WELL! IT'S NOT AS GOOD AS YESTERDAY'S, BUT IT'S BETTER THAN TOMORROW'S…
STAY IN LINE!
HERE
HOW DELICIOUS

SHITHEAD KAPO!
HUM

SAY, IS IT TRUE WHAT THEY TELL US ABOUT OUR FAMILIES?
DOUBT ONLY MAKES YOU LOOK PATHETIC, MY FRIEND.

AUSCHWITZ IS AN EXTERMINATION CAMP. THEY GAS THE OLD PEOPLE AND CHILDREN FIRST.

IN THIS PLACE, MY BOY..

YOU COME IN THROUGH THE DOOR…
YEAH, YEAH— I KNOW THE REFRAIN!

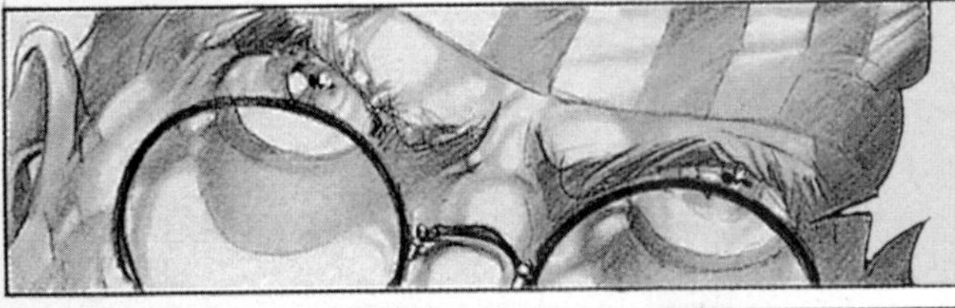
AS YOU SEE, YOU LEARN FAST HERE. HERE THERE ARE NO TOMORROWS. ONLY THE PRESENT COUNTS.

HERE'S SOME ADVICE: TO EAT, KEEP AT THE BACK OF THE LINE, OTHERWISE YOU GET NOTHING BUT WATER. THEY NEVER STIR THE SOUP!

HALT! STOJ!
YOU'RE A PAIN, NEW BOY, THAT'S THE THIRD TIME YOU'VE GOT UP!

MY STOMACH HURTS.
IF YOU'RE SICK, YOU'RE ALREADY DEAD!

16

DAMNED STOMACHACHE!

DAMNED FOOD!

NEARLY THERE…

?...

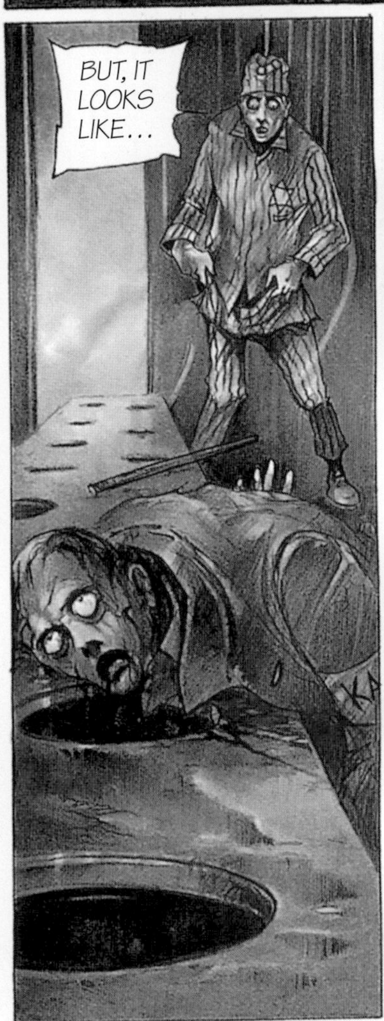
BUT, IT LOOKS LIKE...

THE KAPO!!

?...
ALL MY OWN WORK. I DID HIM IN PERSONALLY.

A KAPO HAS TO BE A JEW-BEATER, OTHERWISE HE HAS NO FUTURE. BUT THIS ONE WAS OVER-ENTHUSIASTIC... LEAVE HIM...

HERE?! BUT THE GERMANS MIGHT FIND HIM!

DON'T WORRY! IT SUITS THEM FINE! WE'VE DONE THEIR JOB FOR THEM.
LET'S NOT HANG AROUND HERE, IT'S NEARLY TIME FOR ROLL CALL.
FLOCK
17

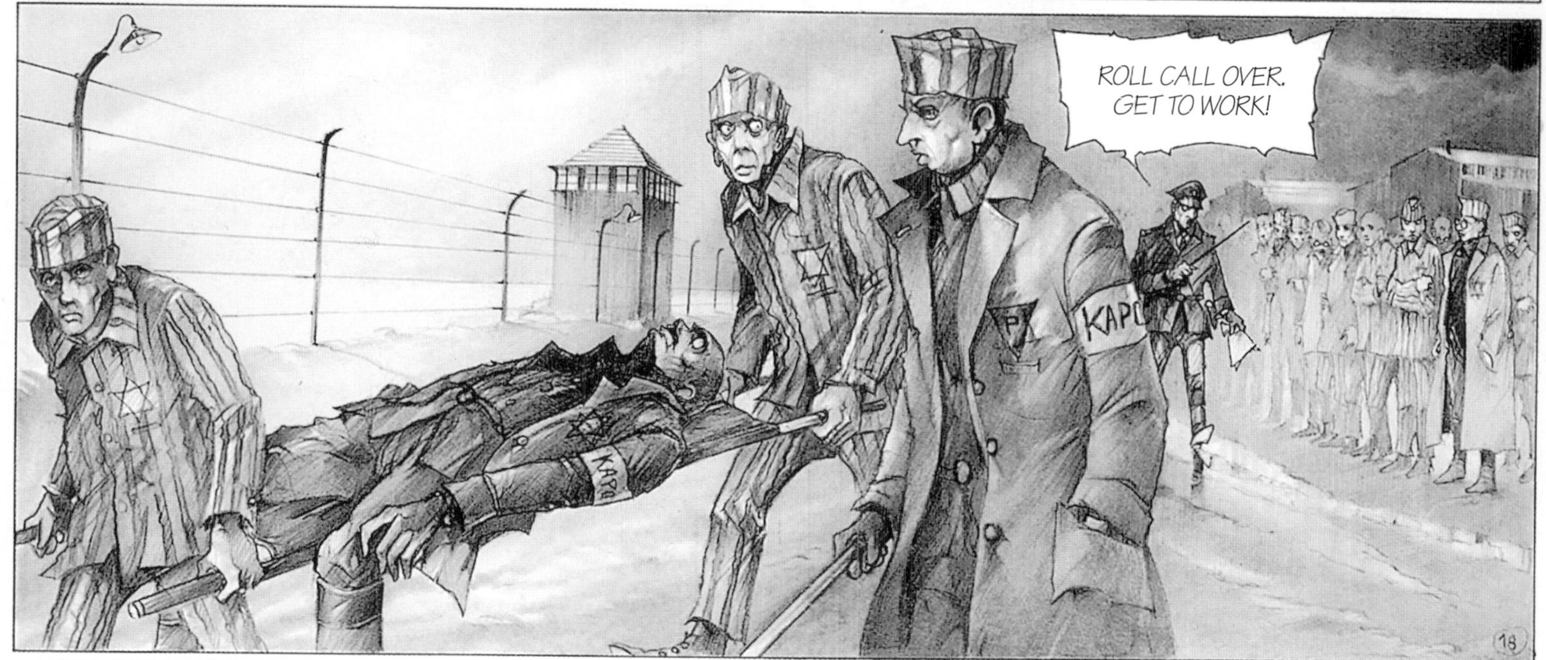

NOTE: THERE WAS NO ROLL CALL BY NAME. IT WAS BY HEAD COUNT.

LAUFSCHRITT

LAUFSCHRITT
SPEED UP!
YOU KNOW, THEY'RE A NATION OF SPORTSMEN.
SHUT UP, YOU TWO!

WHO ARE THOSE PEOPLE ON THE OTHER SIDE?

?!
THEY'RE AN EXCEPTION! IT'S THE FAMILY CAMP, CZECHS FROM THERESIENSTADT. THE MEN, WOMEN, AND CHILDREN ARE ALL TOGETHER. NONE OF THEM HAD THEIR HEADS SHAVED, AND THEY EVEN GOT TO KEEP ALL THEIR BAGGAGE.
AT THE CENTRAL ENROLLMENT OFFICE, I SAW THEY WERE HERE FOR SIX MONTHS QUARANTINE. THEN THEY'RE DOWN FOR "SPECIAL TREATMENT."
SPECIAL TREATMENT?

THAT MEANS THEY GET GASSED.
STOP THAT AT ONCE!

INSTEAD OF THROWING STONES, YOU'D BE BETTER OFF GOING TO SCHOOL!
WE TOLD THEM THEY WERE GOING TO BE ELIMINATED, BUT THEY DIDN'T WANT TO KNOW. THEIR LEADER, HIRSCH, ACCUSED US OF SPREADING PANIC.
?!

WELL, SPEAK OF THE DEVIL...

!
HUM
SO MY DEAR RUDOLF, ANY NEWS OF OUR IMMINENT EXTERMINATION?

YOUR CYNICISM IS MISPLACED, MR. HIRSCH. THIS IS NO LAUGHING MATTER.

I'M NOT LAUGHING! I WOULDN'T DARE MAKE JOKES WITH SUCH A GIFTED MEDIUM AS YOURSELF!

HOW LONG HAVE THEY BEEN HERE?

SIX MONTHS
THE GERMANS ARE SPREADING THE WORD THAT THEY'LL SOON BE TRANSFERRED TO A PLACE CALLED HEYDEBRECK.

GET A MOVE ON!!

ON THIS JOB THEY KEEP US IN SHAPE . . .

AND AS A BONUS, WE GET FRONT ROW SEATS!
YES, I'VE NOTICED.

THE CONVOYS WILL ARRIVE THROUGH THE MAIN GATE.
PERFECT, AND WHEN WILL WE BE READY?
IF YOU INCLUDE THE RAMPS, IT'LL ALL BE FINISHED IN MAY, MEIN STURMBAHNFÜHRER!
21

MY LEG!
GET UP YOU IDIOT!
?
DON'T STOP WORKING!
!?

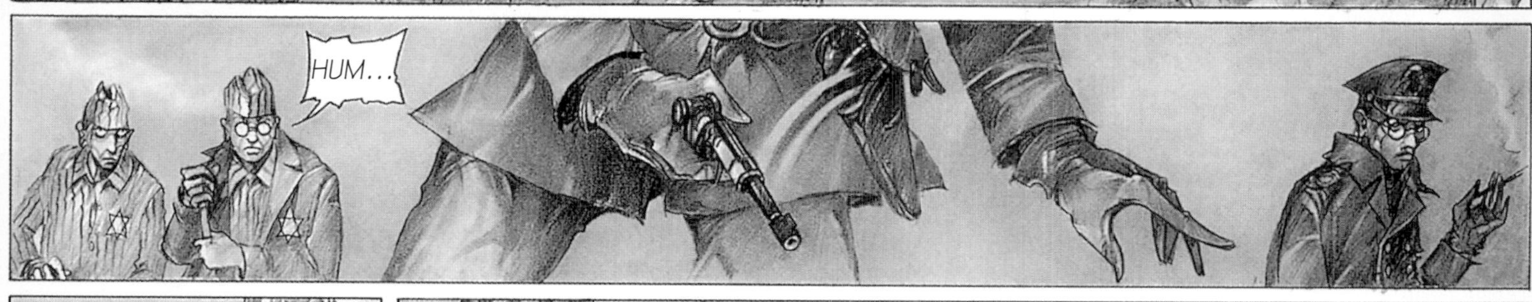

WHAT IS
THIS CIRCUS?

!?
YOUR LETTERS,
PLEASE!

WHAT ARE YOU
DOING HERE,
HIRSCH?
THEY'VE SPLIT US INTO
TWO GROUPS FOR THE
NIGHT. TOMORROW WE'RE
FINALLY LEAVING FOR
HEYDEBRECK...

WHY HAVE THEY
BROUGHT YOU
INTO OUR CAMP?
SO THERE WON'T
BE A CRUSH
WHEN THE
TRUCKS ARRIVE!

WHAT
TRUCKS?
BAH! THE TRUCKS
FOR OUR TRANSFER.
WE'RE NOT WALKING
TO HEYDEBRECK!

DIMITRI,
GIVE THAT
DOLL BACK TO
YOUR SISTER!
NO, IT'S
MINE!
23

COME HERE! I'VE HAD ENOUGH OF YOUR NONSENSE!
IT'S NOT MELANIE'S DOLL!
!?

OH!

I RECOGNIZE IT! IT'S MY DAUGHTER'S.
SHE GAVE IT TO ME...

LIAR! YOU MEAN YOU STOLE IT!
HIRSCH, WHERE IS MY DAUGHTER?
WITH THE OTHER GROUP, I SUPPOSE.

AND MY WIFE?

DO YOU KNOW WHERE SHE IS?
HUM...
THE GERMANS ONLY HAD US TAKE THE KID.

CALM DOWN! WE'LL BE SAFE IN HEYDEBRECK. THEY'VE ASKED US TO WRITE TO OUR FAMILIES TO ADVISE THEM OF OUR TRANSFER.
DIMITRI, IF YOU DON'T STOP...
GO

LATER...
SHALOM.
RABBI, TOMORROW WE'LL CELEBRATE SHABBAT IN HEYDEBRECK.
YOU AGAIN?
I'VE JUST BEEN IN THE CENTRAL OFFICE. THERE'S NOTHING ABOUT ANY TRANSPORT PREPARING TO LEAVE AUSCHWITZ.
COME OVER HERE, I'VE GOT SOMETHING TO SHOW YOU!
IN 48 HOURS YOUR CAMP WILL BE EXTERMINATED! SEE FOR YOURSELF...
A REVOLT IS STILL POSSIBLE..
NO!
KONZENTRATIONSLAGER AUSCHWITZ
Anweisung : 819
6. MAR. 1944
Sonderbefehl : DIE KREMATORIEN RAUMEN ! Nº2 UND 3 FÜR MORGEN. DIE ZIMMER SO SCHNELL WIE MÖGLICH IN ORDNUNG BRINGEN.
MY HEAD IS SPINNING... I NEED TO THINK.
AS YOU LIKE, BUT MAKE YOUR DECISION QUICKLY. THE NIGHT WILL BE SHORT.
25

ANN. .

COME HERE! I WOULDN'T STAY THERE IF I WERE YOU. THEY'LL BE SWITCHING THE CURRENT BACK ON SOON!

I WANT TO GO OVER THERE, I WANT TO SEE MY DAUGHTER, ONE LAST TIME.

THE ONLY WAY TO DO THAT IS TO GET YOURSELF TAKEN ON IN THE SONDERKOMMANDO. THE PROBLEM IS THAT NO ONE COMES BACK ALIVE!

AS FOR ANN . . .

SHE'S JUST AVOIDED MENDELE'S CLUTCHES. HE SOMETIMES USES US AS GUINEA PIGS, THE TORTURER.

STRANGE…IT'S NOT USUALLY THIS QUIET.

DID HE FALL ASLEEP, OR WHAT? I TOLD HIM TO WAIT FOR US IN FRONT OF THE DOOR.

HIRSCH!
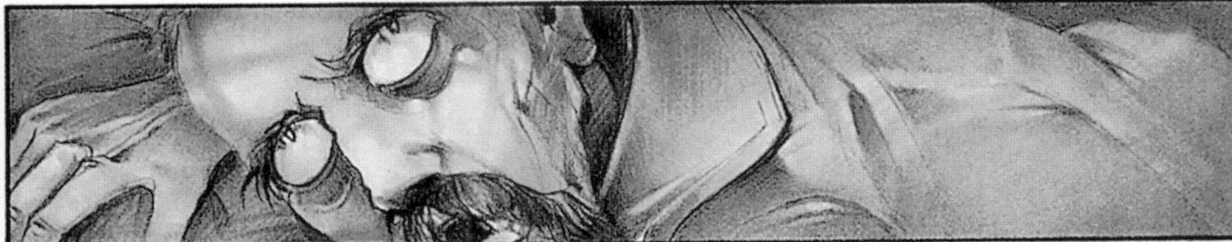

SHALL I CALL A DOCTOR?
TOO LATE. HE'S TAKEN CYANIDE!

WHAT'S ALL THAT NOISE OUTSIDE?
27

THAT'S IT! THEY'RE TAKING THE CZECHS AWAY!
THIS WAY, INTO THE TRUCKS!
WHERE WE'RE GOING, THERE'LL BE SLIDES AND SWINGS!
HOW DO YOU KNOW THAT?
A GERMAN TOLD HIM!

WE ARE GOING TO HEYDEBRECK, AREN'T WE?
YES, MY DEAR LADY. YOU'LL BE EVEN MORE COMFORTABLE THAN HERE...

DIMITRI, HURRY UP, THE TRUCKS ARE LEAVING!
HE'S THE ONE WHO TOLD ME ABOUT THE SLIDES...

IF THEY'RE LEAVING THE CAMP, THE TRUCKS SHOULD TURN RIGHT...

IF THEY TURN LEFT, IT'S JUST A MILE TO THE CREMATORIUM.

29

SOUP'S ON!
...
THIS TIME, DON'T GIVE ME FAULTY MERCHANDISE. I NEED GUYS WITH SOME STRENGTH!

MR. KAZIK, I'LL TAKE YOU AS FAR AS THE ARCH. AFTER THAT YOU'LL BE FREE!

FREE!?
WE ARE NOT AS BAD AS THEY SAY...

WE CAN RECOGNIZE THE GOOD ELEMENTS AMONGST YOU...

AND WHEN WE HAVE TO, WE CAN MAKE AN EXCEPTION!
31

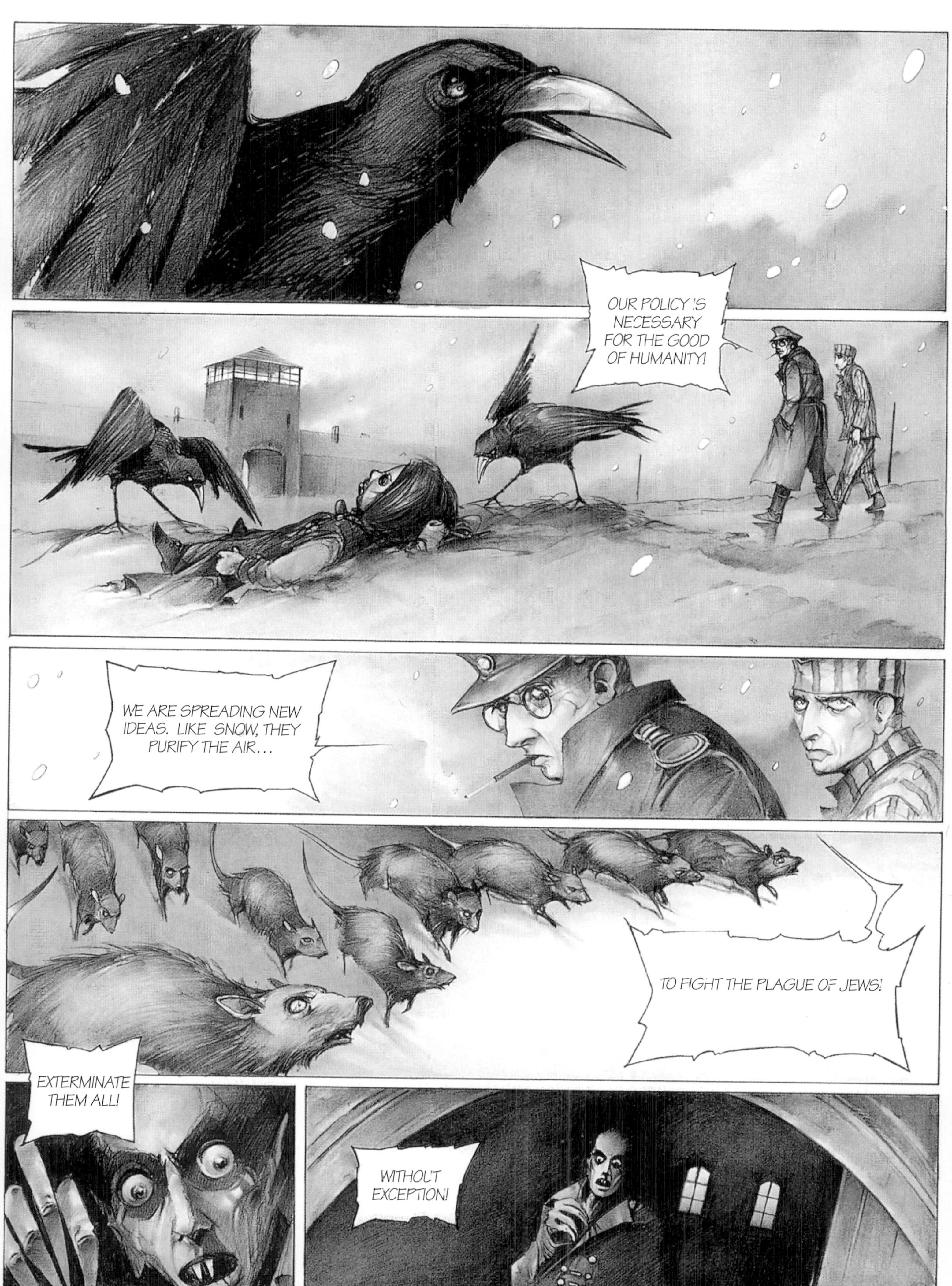
OUR POLICY IS NECESSARY FOR THE GOOD OF HUMANITY!
WE ARE SPREADING NEW IDEAS. LIKE SNOW, THEY PURIFY THE AIR...
TO FIGHT THE PLAGUE OF JEWS!
EXTERMINATE THEM ALL!
WITHOUT EXCEPTION!
32

HEY, MY FRIEND!
JUDEN
VERBOTEN
WAKE UP!!
ARGHH!!!
THE SEDATIVE THEY GAVE YOU LAST NIGHT IS SHIT. YOU MUSN'T TAKE IT!
WHO ARE YOU?
NUMBER 106144, GRAVEDIGGER AT BUNKER 2. I'VE BEEN HERE FOR NEARLY TWO YEARS! I'VE SEEN PLENTY OF FELLAS LIKE YOU…
THEY NEVER STAY LONG…
EVERY TWO OR THREE MONTHS, THEY CHANGE THE TEAM: THEY BRING IN NEW BLOOD AND BURN THE OLD!
33

HOW HAVE YOU SURVIVED?
WITH A FEW FLOWERS HERE AND A FEW FRIEZES THERE…
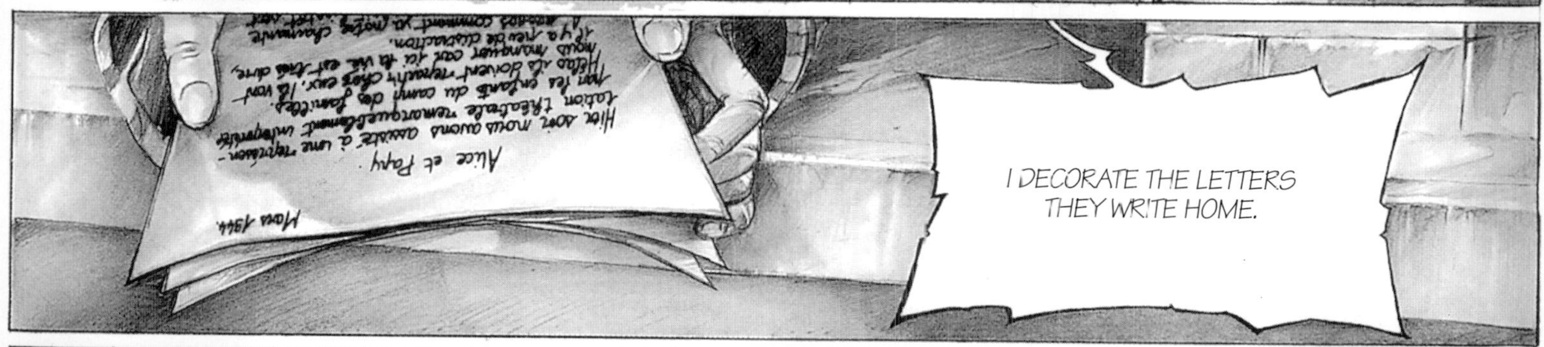
I DECORATE THE LETTERS THEY WRITE HOME.

AND THAT'S ENOUGH TO STAY ALIVE?
COME ON, GET DOWN, THEY'LL BE COMING FOR US IN 10 MINUTES.

BUT?!…
WHAT'S THIS? SOME KIND OF WEIRD FETISH?

IT'S MY DAUGHTER'S! DO YOU THINK I'LL HAVE TIME TO SEE HER?
OF COURSE, AT THE UNDRESSING SESSION WHILE WE'RE PICKING UP THE CLOTHES.
SAY, SHALL WE TAKE HER ON THE JOB WITH US?

YOU HAVE TO IMAGINE THE GAS AS IT STARTS TO TAKE EFFECT, SPREADING BOTTOM TO TOP.
AND IN THE TERRIBLE STRUGGLE THAT ENSUES...
YOU HAVE TO IMAGINE THE LIGHTS GOING OUT IN THE GAS CHAMBER...
IT'S DARK, YOU CAN'T SEE ANYMORE, AND THE STRONGEST STRIVE TO CLIMB HIGHER AND HIGHER...
THEY MUST FEEL THAT THE HIGHER THEY CLIMB, THE MORE AIR THERE WILL BE, AND THE BETTER THEY WILL BREATHE...
35

A BATTLE BREAKS OUT AND EVERYONE RUSHES THE DOOR…

IT'S PSYCHOLOGICAL, THE DOOR IS THERE…

THEY FLING THEMSELVES AT IT AS IF TO BEAT IT DOWN!

IT'S AN IRREPRESSIBLE INSTINCT. IN THIS FIGHT TO THE DEATH, THE CHILDREN AND THE WEAKEST FIND THEMSELVES AT THE BOTTOM, AND THE STRONGEST ON TOP . . .

IN THIS FIGHT TO THE DEATH, THE FATHER CANNOT KNOW IF HIS CHILD IS THERE, CRUSHED BENEATH HIM.

GET READY, WE'RE NEARLY THERE!
EINE LAUS! DEIN TOD!

?!
ONE LOUSE! YOUR DEATH!

NEIN!

TONIGHT ONLY THE MASKS! YOU WON'T NEED THE BAGS!!
?
!

IT'S ALL INSIDE!

THEY MUST HAVE REFUSED TO GET UNDRESSED...

BECAUSE THEY KNEW WHERE THEY WERE...

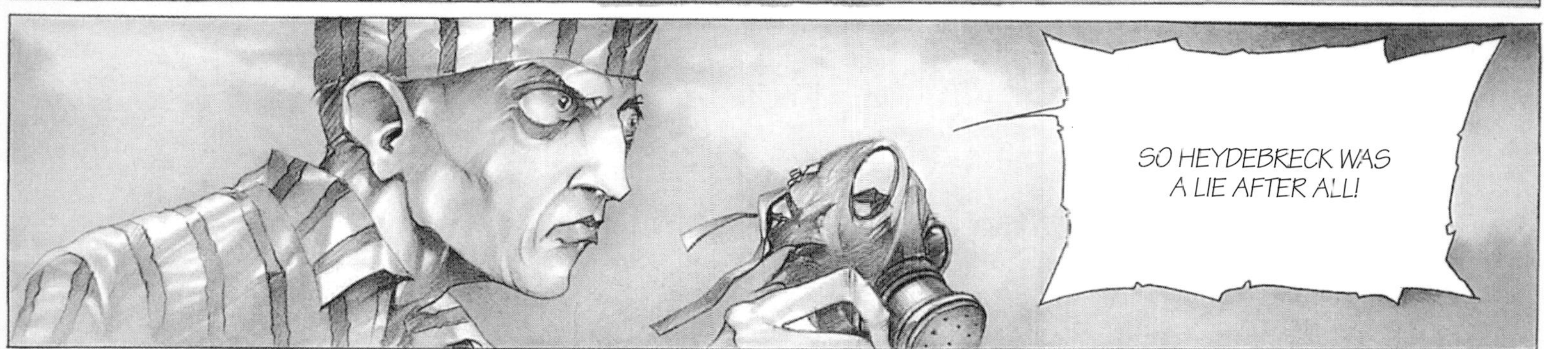

DÉSINFEKTION RAUM

EVERYTHING MUST BE TAKEN DIRECTLY TO THE PIT!

IT'S YOUR TURN TO OPEN THE BALL!

WHERE THE ZYKLON HAD BEEN POURED, THERE WAS NOTHING. WHERE THE CRYSTALS HAD BEEN, THERE WAS NOBODY...
...THE PEOPLE WERE INJURED, FILTHY, BLOODY, BLEEDING FROM THEIR EARS AND NOSES. THEY HAD STRUGGLED AND FOUGHT...
SOME LAY CRUMPLED ON THE GROUND, CRUSHED BEYOND ALL RECOGNITION BY THE WEIGHT OF OTHERS...

CHILDREN WITH THEIR HEADS SPLIT OPEN, VOMIT EVERYWHERE...
...MENSTRUAL BLOOD, TOO, PERHAPS...
NO, NOT PERHAPS, FOR CERTAIN!

THERE WAS EVERY IMAGINABLE THING IN THIS FIGHT FOR LIFE...
THIS FIGHT AGAINST DEATH...

TURN OFF THE VENTILATORS!

LET'S GET ON WITH IT!

KEEP GOING, THERE'S STILL A LOT IN THE BACK!
THERE'S ONE BREATHING OVER THERE!
HURRY UP!

ANN?

AHH...

YOU'RE ALIVE!!
P'PA...

NOTHING LIKE THIS HAS EVER HAPPENED BEFORE!

IT'S A MIRACLE!

IT'S A PROBLEM! WHAT DO WE DO WITH HER NOW?

IT MIGHT WORK IF SHE WERE A FEW YEARS OLDER. BUT SHE'S JUST A CHILD; SHE'D PROBABLY TELL THE FIRST PERSON SHE MET JUST WHERE SHE'S BEEN.
SHE IS THIRTEEN!
IF SHE TALKS ABOUT WHAT SHE'S SEEN, IT WOULD SPREAD LIKE WILDFIRE, AND WE'D PAY FOR IT FOR THE REST OF OUR LIVES.
GIVE HER A CHANCE!
GO BACK TO YOUR POST.
DON'T SEND HER BACK TO DEATH!
I'LL THINK ABOUT IT…
44

HOW MANY
PIECES LEFT?

ABOUT A
HUNDRED!

WHAT! YOU
ASSHOLE,
WHAT'S "ABOUT"
SUPPOSED TO
MEAN?

POUR SOME GAS
OVER THIS PUTRID ROT!

BY THIS EVENING, ALL THIS HAS TO BE ASHES!
SCHNELL!
THEN GET BACK TO THE CREMATORIUM, THERE ARE STILL THINGS TO BE DONE!
46

BUT BEFORE YOU GO, GET RID OF WHAT'S LEFT IN THE OTHER PIT.

IT'S OK, I THINK HE'LL LET HER LIVE!

THE FIRE IS GOOD, IT WARMS YOU UP!

IT DEPENDS ON WHO YOU ARE!
WHAT DO THEY DO WITH THIS?
?
47

HERE, A SOUVENIR!

?!

NOW KEEP WORKING, AND NEVER FORGET: "ARBEIT MACHT FREI!"

...

"WORK MEANS FREEDOM..."

I ESCAPED A MONTH LATER...

EXACTLY A MONTH AFTER BEING LUCKY ENOUGH TO SEE OUR DAUGHTER FOR THE LAST TIME.
HE DID LEAVE HER AT THE CAMP ENTRANCE.

WHAT?!
EXACTLY AS YOU HAD SUG-GESTED...

NOW IT'S YOUR TURN TO LISTEN TO ME!
49

FOR MONTHS, ANN HAD UNDERGONE THE WORST SUFFERING...
SHE HAD SURVIVED THE WORK AND ESCAPED FROM ALL THE SELECTIONS...
UNTIL THAT DAY IN NOVEMBER WHEN FINALLY, WE BECAME PART OF THAT DREADED LOT...
50

HURRY UP!

ONE GROUP HERE!

...AND ANOTHER IN FRONT OF THIS DOOR!

YOU ARE EXCELLENT WORKERS. OUR FACTORIES BENEFIT FROM YOUR SKILL.
SO TODAY WE ARE GOING TO TRANSFER YOU TO ANOTHER CAMP A FEW KILOMETERS FROM HERE...
BUT FIRST OF ALL, GET UNDRESSED, YOU HAVE TO BE DISINFECTED.
YOUR HEALTH IS IMPORTANT TO US!

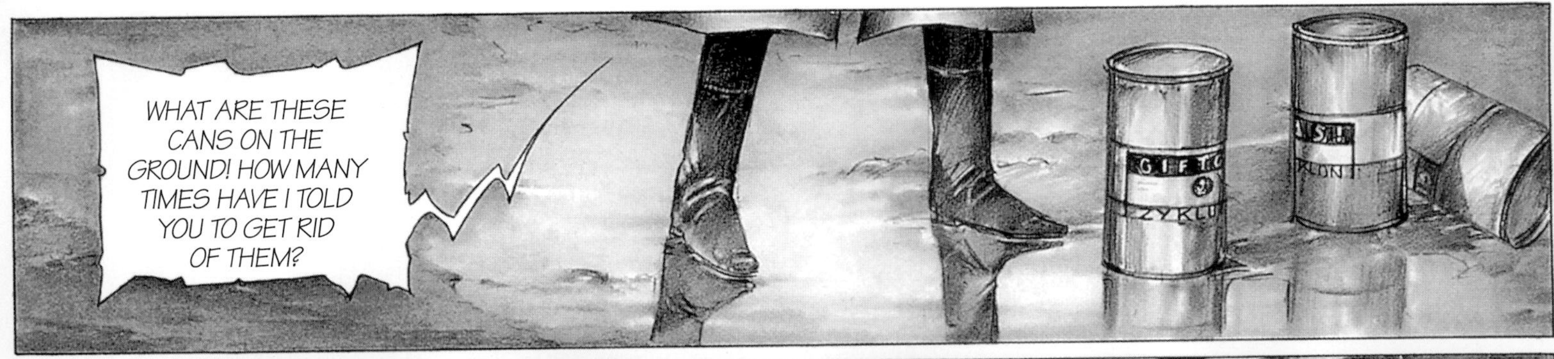
WHAT ARE THESE CANS ON THE GROUND! HOW MANY TIMES HAVE I TOLD YOU TO GET RID OF THEM?

WE ONLY HAVE TWO HANDS, HERR KOMMANDANT!
I WANT IT ALL FINISHED IN TEN MINUTES!

AN ORDER FROM BERLIN, STURMBANNFÜHRER!
?...
...

THEY'VE TAKEN NEW MEASURES...
COULDN'T THIS WAIT?
53

FROM THEN ON, IT WAS FORBIDDEN TO KILL ANYONE INSIDE THE CAMP IN ANY WAY AT ALL. WE WERE GIVEN BLANKETS AND TAKEN BACK TO THE BARRACKS.

RUHE!

54

A FEW DAYS LATER, THEY BLEW UP THE CREMATORIUMS. THEY HAD TO GET RID OF EVERY TRACE OF THEIR CRIMES.
IN MID-JANUARY, THEY SUDDENLY LEFT, DRAGGING BEHIND THEM A GOOD MANY OF US IN THE DEATH MARCHES...

CESSIA!

?
THE BASTARDS!
AVN MÄRZ 9/4
CESSIA, WHERE ARE YOU?
HERE, CLARA!
I'VE FOUND HER...
...SHE'S OVER BY THE CREMATORIUM!
56

!
THERE! IN FRONT OF THE GAS CHAMBER.
SHE HASN'T MOVED.

YISKA DAL VEYISKADASH SH'MAI RABAH…

THIS IS THE PLACE WHERE I DIED…
ANN, YOU MUSTN'T STAY HERE! IT'S TOO DANGEROUS… IT MIGHT COLLAPSE.

COME ON!
57

THEY'VE DESTROYED EVERYTHING. EVERY SCRAP OF PROOF.
WE WILL BEAR WITNESS!

BUT WHO IS GOING TO BELIEVE US?

"THANK YOU, GOD, FOR HAVING MADE US YOUR CHOSEN PEOPLE! BUT PLEASE, COULDN'T YOU HAVE CHOSEN SOMEONE ELSE?"

BLASPHEMING WON'T HELP!
AND WHERE ARE THOSE RUSSIANS? IF IT GOES ON LIKE THIS, WE'LL ALL BE DEAD BY THE TIME THEY ARRIVE! I CAN'T STAND THIS WAR ANY LONGER!

BE PATIENT, THEY CAN'T BE MORE THAN 40 KILOMETERS AWAY; YOU CAN HEAR THE GUNFIRE.
58

IT'S ALL OVER! SOON WE'LL BE ABLE TO GO HOME...

...AND FORGET ABOUT ALL THIS!
WHAT IS IT THAT MAKES THEM ACT THIS WAY?

HATRED.

59

COULDN'T WE JUST HATE EACH OTHER IN PEACE?
68

AND JUST USE WORDS FOR WEAPONS...THE LITTLE ONE IS RIGHT!
THAT'S THE UTOPIAN DREAM OF AN ADOLESCENT WHO'S RUN OUT OF ARGUMENTS. VIOLENCE WILL ALWAYS REIGN SUPREME!
"LOVE ONE ANOTHER" IS MORE OF A CHRISTIAN IDEAL THAN A JEWISH ONE.
WHO CAN ACCEPT HIS NEIGHBOR WHOLEHEARTEDLY, WITHOUT DIFFERENCE, WITHOUT SUSPICION? WE CAN'T BE INFALLIBLE.
IT'S INEVITABLE.
AND IN EXTREME TIMES LIKE THIS, PROBLEMS ARE ALWAYS SOLVED IN THE SAME WAY! THROUGH SILENCE OR VIOLENCE!
BUT WHERE DOES THIS HATRED COME FROM?
FROM OUR FRUSTRATIONS.

SO WHY DON'T WE TRY TO UNDERSTAND WHERE THE HATRED COMES FROM BEFORE FIGHTING IT?
DOES THAT MEAN FORGIVING PEOPLE LIKE HITLER?
?
DO YOU THINK THAT A TYRANT LIKE HITLER JUST APPEARS BY MAGIC OUT OF SOME DIABOLICAL BLACK HAT? NOT AT ALL. AS FAR AS I KNOW, ALL HUMAN BEINGS STARTED OFF AS CHILDREN, AND NO CHILD IS BORN A TYRANT...
ANN IS VERY WEAK... SHE WAS SICK AGAIN LAST NIGHT.
PROBABLY A STOMACH BUG.
THE IMPORTANT THING IS THAT SHE SLEEPS...
...SHE'LL FEEL BETTER IN THE MORNING.
62

BALUCKI RYNEK SQUARE. DO YOU KNOW THE PLACE, CLARA?

YES, UNFORTUNATELY...

IT'S WHERE I USED TO BUY HER GOLDFISH...

63

LOOK, THERE ARE BIRDS ON HER GRAVE!

YOU MUST BE MISTAKEN, CLARA ...

...THERE HAVE NEVER BEEN BIRDS AT BIRKENAU.

...

ANN DIED OF TYPHUS JUST TWO DAYS BEFORE THE CAMP WAS LIBERATED...

KAZIK, I CAN HEAR FOOTSTEPS ON THE OTHER SIDE!

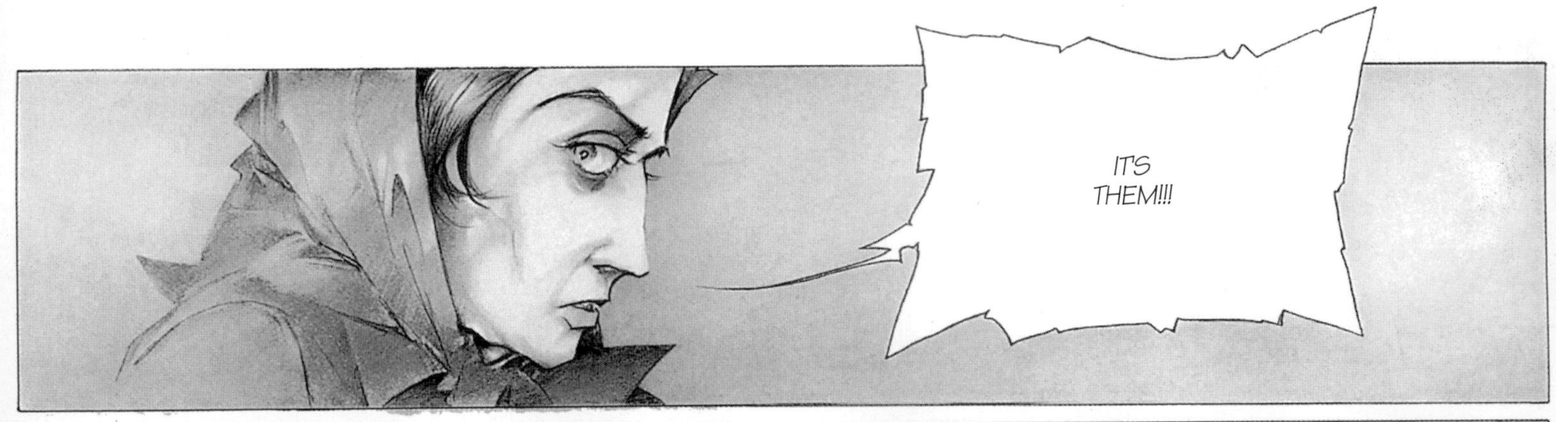
IT'S THEM!!!

KLICKKKIK KKK
...
THIS TIME, IT'S OUR TURN!

OUTSIDE, OLD FOLKS!
WE'RE BOTH GOING.
WE WANT TO DIE TOGETHER, IT'S OUR RIGHT!

DO WHAT YOU'RE TOLD!

BIND THEIR HANDS!
WE DON'T WANT TO BE TIED UP!
COME ON, THE OTHER ONE!
DON'T TIE US UP, IT'S SHAMEFUL, LEAVE ME ALONE!
SHUT UP!
YOU'RE BREAKING MY HAND, LET ME GO!
ALL THESE DEATHS ARE YOUR FAULT! OUR COLLEAGUES, OUR BROTHERS!
WE HAVE THE RIGHT–
WHY ARE YOU TYING US UP? THEY'VE LIED TO YOU!
NO ONE CAN LIE TO US ANY MORE!
66

ACCUSED OF BEING TRAITORS,
KAZIK AND CESSIA
WERE EXECUTED ON
OCTOBER 26, 1993,
IN A BARRACKS
NEAR TUZLA, BOSNIA.
67

EPILOGUE

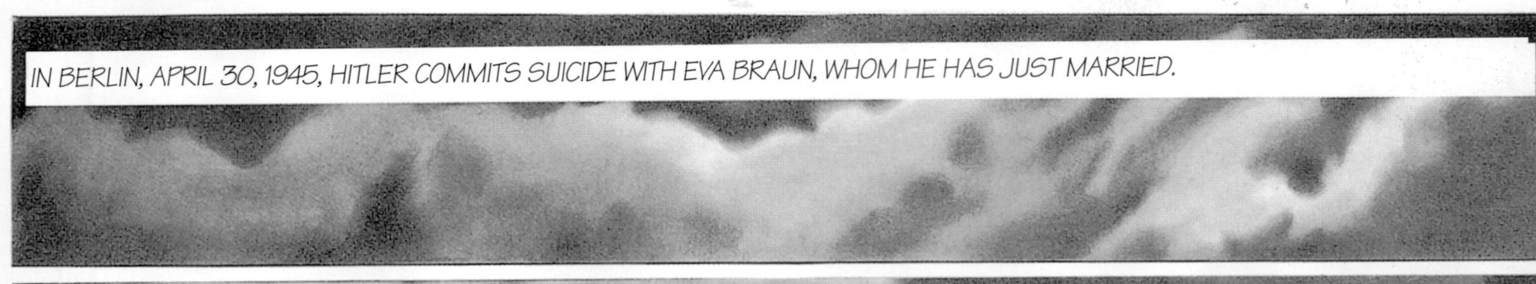

MAY 7, 1945: THE NAZI CAPITULATION IS SIGNED IN A SCHOOLROOM IN REIMS, FRANCE.
MAY 8, 1945: THE OFFICIAL SIGNATURE TAKES PLACE IN BERLIN.

AUGUST 6, 1945: AN ATOMIC BOMB IS DROPPED ON HIROSHIMA.
AUGUST 9, 1945: AN ATOMIC BOMB IS DROPPED ON NAGASAKI.

NOVEMBER 20, 1945: THE NUREMBERG WAR CRIMES TRIALS BEGIN. THEY LAST 351 DAYS.
POST-AUSCHWITZ, THERE IS STILL NO SHORTAGE OF PEOPLE WHO KILL OTHER PEOPLE. OTHER CRIMES AGAINST HUMANITY, NO DOUBT, ARE WAITING TO HAPPEN.

BACKGROUND INFORMATION

For a long time, depicting the Shoah, or Holocaust, in a work of graphic fiction seemed unthinkable. But ever since the TV series *Holocaust*, and later Steven Spielberg's film *Schindler's List*, fictional accounts of this painful period in history are increasingly more common, representing the deeply personal visions of their creators, and not necessarily those of history books. This is true of films like Roberto Benigni's *Life Is Beautiful* and Emmanuel Finkiel's *Journeys*. A precedent for fictionalizing the period can be seen in the book *Maus* by Polish-born American Art Spiegelman. In his graphic novel, Spiegelman tells the story of his parents' deportation to Auschwitz, where the Jews are portrayed as mice, and the Nazis as cats. Pascal Croci's treatment of Auschwitz is less symbolic. There is no key to understanding what provoked his decision to create this moving story, but rather pieces of a puzzle. In the following pages, the author aims to help readers discover how the pieces fit together through an interview about how the project came about. The interview is also an opportunity to explain some of the script's less obvious elements, and to reveal the complicity between the author and various witnesses he met during the conception and creation of this work.

Françoise Sylvie Pauly

WHY A GRAPHIC NOVEL ABOUT AUSCHWITZ?

Pascal Croci: When I was ten, I was struck by the emblematic image of the camp in a TV documentary, *The Gates of Hell*. I didn't understand what it was about. It scared me...the whole building disturbed me. It all looked so gloomy; on the tower you could see two dark openings, just over the porch. They looked like a pair of eyes...What intrigued me was that entrance, the light, and the terrible secrets I was sure were hidden inside. But when I asked, the only answer I got from my family was "You're too young to understand..." This graphic novel reflects my quest for answers about the subject.

I remember that everything started with Claude Lanzmann's *Shoah*. The wealth of witnesses in his documentary made me certain that a graphic novel could tell the story of everyday life in the camp of Auschwitz-Birkenau.

Added to this were my own questions about death. It was nothing morbid, just the sort of philosophical questions which every normal person should ask at some time during his life. Maybe I also wanted to exorcise an unconscious fear, because the house we lived in at Seine-et-Marne had been requisitioned during the war by the German army. My studio was next to the room that had been the officers' mess. When the allies arrived, a German officer killed himself with a bullet through his head!

Was there anything else that pushed you into taking the plunge?
The deciding factor was in 1993 during an exhibition of drawings by deportees in the town hall of the 11th arrondissement in Paris. I was struck by a pencil sketch that had been made on the back of concentration camp administrative forms. The drawing showed a fence whose shadow was visible on the ground; the light obviously came from a watchtower... While I was looking at it, an old lady came up to me and started telling me about her journey to hell. Her number was tattooed on her arm! That day, I had found my first witness. After this vital meeting had taken place, I got in touch with members of the "Friends of Auschwitz." I knew that I was taking an enormous risk, but to have done nothing, to have said nothing, it would have been impossible for me.

How did the deportees react when you told them of your project?
I must say that at the beginning, most of them were reticent. Then when I showed them my first sketches, it must have broken the ice, because some of them agreed to tell me about what they had lived through.
I think what interested them was that a non-Jew and "stranger to the Shoah" should write something about their experience.

Was it a witness who suggested one of the most harrowing scenes in the album, where Kazik discovers his daughter still alive in the gas chamber ?
No, what happened to Kazik and his daughter came to me from a true story told by Christian Bernadac in his book *Les Mannequins nus* (*The Naked Mannequins*). A witness tells how a young Transylvanian girl was found alive in the gas chamber. This miracle came about because her face fell against the damp concrete floor. This dampness prevented the Zyklon B gas from being activated, so she was not asphyxiated. For a quarter of an hour, the German officers didn't know what to do with her—I mention this in my dialogue—a Hungarian doctor in the sonderkommando gave her injections so she would be able to escape. But the Germans were worried that she would talk of what she had seen, so they shot her in the head.

Did you purposely "humanize" some of the Germans? I'm thinking in particular of the scenes with the doll and the dream.
No, or if I did, I did so unconsciously. I was simply drawing attention to the fact that several types of ignominious characters can coexist; on one hand there is the perverse officer, on the other a more administrative one. They use different methods, but the end result is the same. When the officer gives Kazik back the doll, one could almost think he has a human side. But by not letting on that he has saved the girl, he remains perverse and arrogant. Can there be anything worse for a father than not knowing what has happened to his child?!

It is surprising that Kazik manages not to crack.
This type of psychological torture was common currency in the camps. The deportees knew that the slightest sign of weakness meant execution. Some had a more highly developed sense of self-preservation than others.

Your work shows everyday life in the camp. What happened during a "typical" day?
There was no such thing as a typical day. The deportees never worked twice in the same place. This is well illustrated in *Schindler's List* when Schindler asks the servant girl about the German officer's reactions. The prisoners' world was one of permanent insecurity. They never knew what tomorrow would bring. I tried to bring out this insecurity in my story, through its uneven rhythm, and through alternating the points of view of Kazik and Cessia.

Did values such as friendship and solidarity exist within the camp?
My witnesses confirm this. In the most terrible situations, they tried to counterbalance reality with happy memories. When the men couldn't manage to sleep, they told jokes; the women exchanged recipes... This may seem surrealist, but all of them clutched at elements of real life to "escape" from the horror of the camp.

Why did you make the episode of the family camp central to your story?
I wanted to use this exceptional example as an illustration of the pathway toward death. When the Czechs from the Therensienstadt ghetto arrived in Auschwitz in 1944, they kept their luggage with them and were not separated from their families. There was even a school inside their camp, and it was used by the Germans as a theater in the evenings. These Czechs were privileged. They couldn't think of themselves as being like the other Jews. In the story, the children talk about swings and slides. This is not what they actually said, but I can imagine that this is how they must have felt. Suddenly, this life which was practically "normal," was plunged into horror. One historian disliked my symbolic approach and the fact that I had used an exception to convey a general situation. The "special camp" was first mentioned by Philip Muller, one of the witnesses in Lanzmann's *Shoah*. To my astonishment, some of my witnesses knew nothing of the special camp's existence. That is why I chose to introduce the dramatic story of the Czechs into my story.

Did the Czechs really think they would not go to the gas chambers?
If you consider the context, it is understandable. Auschwitz-Birkenau was organized into sub-camps, and in each complex there were Russian, Hungarian, Gypsy, and Jewish prisoners. They were not all bound for the same fate. If you were part of a community which had been left alone for six months, it was only human nature that you would start to let your guard down. In reality, that is exactly how it happened. Hirsch, their leader, had never wanted to believe in the final solution. When he realized his mistake, he preferred to kill himself.

Of all the violence perpetrated by the Nazis, which type seems to you the most abominable?
The gas chambers, without a doubt!

In your opinion, can the lack of revolt be explained?
Unbearable fear is at the root of an absence of revolt. After crossing half of Europe in cattle cars, rebellion was no longer possible. That is why I often show faces with huge desperate eyes. The Nazis controlled the camp through a reign of terror. By taking away the Jews' own identity, they made them see that human dignity and law no longer existed. I wonder if it was not this terrible dehumanization which enabled them to lead the Jewish people to the gas chambers so easily. The Nazi doctrine and its application, that's the great evil my drawings are denouncing.

Did anyone ever come back alive from the sonderkommandos?
The Germans didn't leave embarrassing witnesses behind their crimes. If my character manages to survive in the sonderkommando for two years, it is only because he decorates the German soldiers' letters. This painter is not an invention. His name was David Olère, who really existed. On the character's prison uniform in the book, I reproduced his real camp number.

THE HISTORICAL TRUTH

Does your graphic novel contain a philosophical message?
Yes. The persecution of the Jews throughout history has led me to think about religion. Christianity teaches people to "Love one another." In my opinion, this is a delusion! To avoid another Auschwitz, we have to face up to the contradictions at the heart of human nature. It isn't utopian to think that we can "hate each other in peace." When I make Ann say this (page 67), the words are not hers but mine.
What I propose may seem rather drastic, but it results from my deepest convictions. If you compare what religious programs say to the actual discourse that goes on in private within Christian, Muslim, and Jewish communities, the contrast is so great that it makes any true brotherly love impossible! My story tells of the power religion has to separate people. Members of each side think they own the truth, and they want to convince the other side that they are right—that is what is so dangerous!

In creating this graphic novel about the Shoah, you haven't taken the easy way out. Are you aware that, on top of that, such a commentary on the subject can be disturbing?
The role of a book is to unveil elements that have been swept under the carpet. The recent controversy over the film *Life Is Beautiful* shows that this is a delicate subject, and that feelings still run close to the surface. Of course, I am aware that what I say may be misinterpreted, or twisted... That's the risk you take when you refuse to use clichés. My drawings and dialogues are not exactly ambiguous. I offer the reader the essence of what is happening, and they discover, along with the story's protagonists, the enormity of the crimes the Nazis committed.
For a long time the Second World War has been presented as a completely black-and-white situation. I have broken with this over-simplified version of history. I wanted to show that there were nuances on both sides and in both communities.

Preparatory sketch

If we follow your reasoning to its logical conclusion, you would find the Jewish kapos guilty, but find Germans who saved deportees innocent?
No, there is no possible forgiveness of the Nazis. And I would go even further than that... I think that they were not the only guilty parties. Hitler and the people we all know about, such as Barbie and Papon, were not the only ones responsible. There are still Nazis hiding among us now, in South America and in Europe. The silence that surrounds this fact bothers me. As for the Jews, I want to give a true picture of my witnesses, by showing them as they behaved toward each other in the camp: some were little bosses, some naive, others were strong, and still others saintly...

What about heroes?
I don't know if we can call them heroes... A witness told me that once a deportee escaped from a train, and the Germans shot ten people at random in reprisal. Is it heroic to think of oneself first and not of the consequences that escaping might have for the others? I'm neither a historian or a documentarian, but I have tried to reconstitute the regularity of these events as faithfully as possible.

Nevertheless, your book is fiction...
Apart from the imaginary couple, Kazik and Cessia, my story strictly follows the course of history. Every incident inside the camp actually happened: the elimination of the Czechs in the family camp, the construction of the ramp, the epidemics during the time of the Liberation...
I set myself a strict timeline: Kazik arrived at Auschwitz March 5, 1944; on the seventh of March, the Czechs were exterminated. Kazik's escape corresponds to that of Rudolf Vbra, told in Lanzmann's *Shoah*. My story is also full of the type of everyday details that historians find less interesting.

On this subject, do the contradictions between fiction and reality bother you?
Art Spiegelman did it before me, and no one blamed him for "novelizing" his parents' memories. I'm not making a documentary, I've got nothing to prove. I'm using a story to recount a historical episode. It seems to me that the graphic novel form is, in fact, an excellent medium for explaining how the Nazis put the final solution into action.

There is something else that strikes the reader: why did you connect Auschwitz with the events in the former Yugoslavia?
Because of certain worrying similarities. The pictures of the Yugoslavian camps showed us emaciated people who were about to disappear. I immediately thought of the Nazi death camps. It was also very important for me to connect this story to the reality of today...so that Auschwitz doesn't remain just a thing of the past.

In that case, why call the book *Auschwitz*?
My witnesses would have preferred me to use a more symbolic name. But I wanted to keep this title. When you talk about Auschwitz-Birkenau, you mean a concentration complex near the Polish village of Oswiecim. My story happens in a precise area: in the family camp and certain barracks, namely B2B, B2A, and maybe B2C, and in the women's camp, which was on the other side of the railroad tracks.

LEST WE FORGET

In the story, Kazik thinks he knows everything about his wife...
For 48 years, the couple survived above all because of their silence. Before their execution in former Yugoslavia, they finally had to tell each other the truth; they had to go back to the time when they went through "almost" the same thing...

They also tell this story so that no one will forget what happened.
They pay their due to memory. Even if Cessia seems reticent at first...because it is very difficult to say such terrible things to a person one loves. Kazik learns how his daughter was saved by a German officer, and then died of typhoid two days before the camp was liberated.

Preparatory sketch

Who was your inspiration for your main character?
The real Kazik is not the one in the story. His name is in homage to my principal witness, Mr. Kazimierz Kac, who entered Auschwitz when he was 41. He already had a life, a wife, and two children. I could have used Charles Baron, another witness whose stories really affected me. But I wanted the main character to be Polish, to insist on the fact that Auschwitz was in Poland and not in Germany! The first Jews to be exterminated were the Poles. This explains why so few survived. Kazimierz is really exceptional! As for the fictional character, he is a mixture of several witnesses and several people who actually existed.

What about Cessia?
Cessia really is the name of Kazimierz's wife. As soon as they arrived in Auschwitz, they were separated. I wanted to pay tribute here to this woman who he has continued to love since her death, two days before the liberation of the Stutthof camp.

How much of this book is directly related to what the witnesses told you?
The arrival of the train is directly inspired by their stories, along with the reception committee, those deportees who had to pick up the personal belongings of the arrivals in order to take them to be sorted in the Kanada barrack. It was precisely at that moment that the long-termers would try to separate mothers from their children to prevent their being sent to the gas chambers. The Nazis first eliminated those who were not of an age to work. That meant that the population of the camp started at fifteen. Archives found by the Russians show that when the Nazis spared babies and children, it was only to use them for experiments.

Character studies

Preparatory sketch

THE NARRATIVE

It was not easy to write a story that takes place in an enclosed space. I wanted to show not only the men's camp, but also the women's. With the Czechs who were quarantined for six months in the family camp, I had found a storyline. Otherwise, I was free to invent the narrative. I had no constraints and no particular number of pages. It was very pleasant to work in such conditions. To write this story, I excluded any document (books, films, photos) that didn't originate from Auschwitz. My main source of inspiration was Claude Lanzmann's *Shoah*, as well as photos in the collection of the AFMA (Association Foundation of the Memory of Auschwitz). Since I couldn't take them away, I went to exhibitions and made quick sketches which I would rework at home. One image that particularly struck me while I was doing my research was the one which showed bulldozers filled with corpses. It is to me the emblem of the horror that grew out of the Nazi ideology. *Schindler's List* was also a reference for my work. In my opinion, it is the most successful work of fiction about the Shoah. Thanks to this film, I think it is possible to talk differently about the Holocaust. Spielberg raised people's awareness.

AVOIDING AESTHETICISM IN THE DRAWINGS

I wanted a finished product that would be realistic, in black and white, without special effects or style. My first problem, even more than the historical reconstitution, was how to avoid voyeurism. I wanted to avoid the perverse effects of fixed images of nudity. That is why bodies are always shown as corpses, decomposed… For the same reasons, I made no visual representation of the gas ovens. I preferred to put myself in the shoes of a deportee who sees the smoke and who is always surrounded by the odor of death. As for the scene when the corpses are found in the gas chamber, both the character and the reader feel crushed by this incredible vision of horror.

When I start working on a board, it's never with a feeling of pleasure. It is complicated to do a realistic drawing. You have to pay attention to the perspective, to the characters' faces, to the historical details. I was also worried about reproducing the same images over and over. There is mist everywhere; the atmosphere is always heavy. I didn't want to show the horizon so that the reader would have the feeling of penetrating a world outside time. This symbolic representation is close to how the witnesses remember things. For them, Auschwitz is a cold, misty place where death reigns. Graphically speaking, I was not faithful to certain historical details, like the guns, for example.

THE THREE MAIN WITNESSES: RENEE ESKENAZ

e witnesses; were there any difficult moments?

With my witnesses I have a relationship of trust and respect. Even if it may not be easy to tell someone about what one went through at Auschwitz, the fact that we met often meant that we became closer. It wasn't an impersonal experience, like answering a journalist's questions. Renée Eskenazi told me that she was sure she would say things in a private conversation that she would not say in front of a camera or on the telephone. If you speak in front of a TV crew, there is the risk that what you say will be taken out of context and distorted. I noticed that in general, my witnesses seemed disturbed when I asked them technical questions: "Before the ramp was constructed, through which gate did you enter Auschwitz?" The problem is that some witnesses wanted to impose their own memories as the only true record of the period. The witnesses from Auschwitz had never heard of the family camp. When they didn't want to believe in its existence, I explained that the story did not come from me, but from eyewitnesses in Claude Lanzmann's film.

Were there any questions that you did not feel you could ask?

I didn't want to censor myself and have taboos. I asked my questions freely, even though they were sometimes very painful. On first approach, the interrogation "Did you ever joke around?" can seem indecent. But I always explained to my witnesses beforehand why I was asking such things. There were no hidden agendas behind my questions, and I wasn't trying to cause them pain. For them, it was a form of therapy. Talking about a painful experience may help to get over it. But what they lived through as deportees is not something they can forget. There is always, and will always be, a crack deep inside their being, a pain which they can never overcome. Listening to Charles Baron, I realized that he had lived his whole life with the war, and that the Nazis had robbed him of his youth. Out of respect, not everything could be told in this book.

What was their reaction to the finished work?

Charles Baron knows this medium very well, because his daughter, Annie Baron-Carvais, wrote a book on the subject of graphic novels. As for the other witnesses, apart from some difficulties because they were not used to reading comic strips, they had no criticism either of the content or the story line. In fact this lack of comments wasn't really what I expected. I thought they might be reticent about certain passages, but nothing I had written seemed to shock them. Their remarks had more to do with their own personal memories. They wanted to recognize themselves in the prisoners' uniforms, and that posed a problem for me. I only had documentation about the shirts and the trousers, so I added a cap from my imagination. Mr. Baron informed me later that the deportees did not wear this sort of headgear, but a flat beret [see page 81, Charles Baron's letter to Croci on this subject]. The problem was that I couldn't manage to draw this beret. My deportees looked ridiculous. So, because I found it graphically more acceptable, I chose to keep my imaginary headgear, and therefore did not respect historical detail for the costume! I did the same thing with the Nazis, who, except in case of alert, did not wear helmets in Auschwitz: they wore military berets instead. Strangely enough, my witnesses completely understood this symbolic choice applied to the Germans, but not when it was applied to the deportees.

If you had just one message to convey?

That the story of the deportation is relevant to us all. After exterminating the Jews, the Germans would have attacked other peoples. In any case, history belongs to everyone, Jewish or not. No one has the right to keep such serious events from the rest of society. While I was writing this story, I paid more attention than usual to what I heard around me in cafés, in the street, or on the TV. I came to the conclusion that it wasn't only Le Pen* and his fanatics who are dangerous! I brought out this book for all those who lack the sensitivity to understand, all those people whose irresponsible remarks enable other genocides to take place.

*French politician with extreme right-wing and often racist views.

Should we forgive the Germans?

It is not for me to judge. But I think that the Nazi violence is beyond forgiveness.

To conclude, how did your family react while you were working on this subject?

In fact it was other people who asked me if I managed to sleep. I would answer that I had no problem sleeping, because I hadn't actually lived through the period. On the other hand, Lucie, my girlfriend's daughter, who is eleven years old, asked me questions about the drawings. She borrowed Art Spiegelman's *Maus* from her school library. I answered her questions. I think it is healthy, not morbid, to talk about the final solution. It is necessary to educate, to talk about these things seriously so that they never happen again. That is why I wrote this book, so that it could be read by adults as well as by children.

Preparatory sketch

HARLES BARON, AND KAZIMIERZ KAC

A LETTER FROM RENÉE ESKENAZI

"You wanted to have the feelings of someone who was deported to Auschwitz-Birkenau as a preface or an illustration to the book you are writing. It is not easy to sum up everything in one sentence: so many images cascade before my eyes. The arrival in Birkenau is a nightmare, a vision of a hell within hell. Every day of my life, I have Auschwitz in the background. Then fifty years after my return, in painful silence, I see my mother in a halo of human dignity, as she kisses me for the last time. This was her farewell to her three children.

"Thank you Pascal, for the task you have accomplished. However, you have to know that all the characters that you have imagined cannot possibly convey the reality we lived through. Too many atrocities have made orphans of us. For my part, I wish you every happiness for the future.

In loving friendship, Renée Eskenazi"

RENÉE ESKENAZI is retired. She now lives in the 11th arrondissement of Paris. At the age of 17, she was deported with her family to the camp of Auschwitz-Birkenau. She escaped from the gas chamber with her sister.

AN EYEWITNESS ACCOUNT FROM CHARLES BARON

You ask: "Which of the images you took away from Auschwitz had the strongest effect on you?" There are many, but because your book speaks of the children who, so many years after my liberation, continue to haunt me not only at night, but also during my waking hours...

"It is nighttime. Glimmers of light from camouflaged lamps punctuate the darkness. Suddenly, the dark is torn apart as if by a huge flame, and the darkness disappears, swallowed up by an intensely harsh white light. All the spotlights have been turned onto the road adjoining the camp. From beyond the central watchtower, through the gate that leads to death, a group is approaching, growing more discernible as it draws nearer. At the center of the group are children, around ten or twelve years old. They are wearing long white nightgowns that hang down around their feet. A gang of SS in khaki parade uniforms surrounds them, pointing machine guns at these unfortunate "undermen," most likely survivors from the August arrivals. In slow motion, the abominable cortege passes before the long brick building, they walk in front of us, to avoid the barbed wire. This is a nightmare parade with only one end, as both organizers and witnesses know. They are being led toward the most horrible death: slow asphyxiation in a gas chamber specifically designed for the purpose. Beside me, Russian officers sniff. One of them is crying silently, repeating over and over again: 'They look like angels...they look like angels...' Angels they were indeed, but angels entering hell."

Letter from Charles Baron Clarifying the "Beret" Issue »

Charles Baron

Mr. Pascal Croci

Dear Sir,

You have asked me many questions—as you have to my fellow deportees—about my experience in the concentration camp of Auschwitz-Birkenau and other Nazi camps. I have answered you with the utmost frankness about what I saw and went through from September 1942 to April 1945, and I have always avoided telling you about anything which I did not witness personally, or in which I was not directly involved. I have authorized you to quote from my declarations should you wish to do so, provided that you do not in any way change or misinterpret my words.

You recently sent me the proofs of drawings for your book "Auschwitz-Birkenau" for my comments before publication. I thus felt able to ask you to rectify certain elements, concerning both the form and the underlying message of your work.

I am therefore surprised that you have ignored a remark which I made at the outset of our conversations: you have shown the prisoners wearing a military style of beret, and not the round, blue-and-white-striped, flat beret which they in fact wore at the time. I find it hard to understand your logic, since in every other aspect you have shown your desire to fully comprehend every detail concerning the tragedy of the Shoah, in order to better convey the period through a popular artistic medium.

Consequently, it seems to me that the change in atmosphere evoked, at least in my eyes, by the military-style head dress, gives grounds to change or modify the title of your book, in order to make it more coherent with your personal vision.

I hereby send you back your proofs with my best regards.

Ch Baron

CHARLES BARON was born in Paris in July 1926, of a French mother and a Polish father. He was deported to Auschwitz on September 18, 1942. Being "apt for work," he was employed in several camps as logger, aviation factory worker, etc. He managed to escape with other deportees in April 1945, but returned to France only on September 17, 1945. Since 1986, Charles Baron has been retired from his job with a medical equipment company. He lives today with his wife, in close contact with their two daughters and grandchildren. He is the former vice general secretary of the Friends of Auschwitz Society, which is involved in keeping alive memories of the camp. Charles Baron is a regular participant on radio and television, but what he likes best is giving direct explanations to children during school visits.

KAZIMIERZ KAC (KAZIK)

Born: March 1, 1903, Lodz. Marries Cessia April 20, 1928. Birth of a daughter in 1929. Lives in Lodz until 1942.

In the Lodz ghetto in 1940, the Germans hang five Jews in Balucki Rynek Square. Kazik witnesses the scene. He knows the square well; it was where he used to buy his goldfish when he was a boy...

Auschwitz-Birkenau: during a selection in the shower room, he miraculously escapes from the experiments of Dr. Mengele.

Cessia dies in Stutthof, two days before the camp is liberated. Their daughter is gassed at Auschwitz.

1999: Kazik at his home in Paris. There are photos on the living room wall. One of the photos is of Cessia.

Kazik is different from all the other witnesses. Most of them were fairly young when they were deported. After the war, they were able to rebuild their lives, have a family...

Not Kazik. His life stopped at Auschwitz. You only have to see his face when he looks at his wife's photo... His silence is the silence of suffering.

REFERENCES AND INSPIRATIONS

Preparatory sketch

Nosferatu (1922) — F. W. Murnau's film is seen by some critics as a form of pre-Nazi propaganda. The rats spread the plague, the rat symbolizing the Jew...

In 1942 in Warsaw, children would escape from the ghetto in search of food for their families. The Germans made a sport out of shooting them down. They called this "rat hunting."

Three doll studies

The Doll — I had the idea of the doll when I saw the title of a book by Christian Bernadac, *The Naked Mannequins.*

One day at an exhibition of the Association Foundation Memory of Auschwitz, while I was reviewing photos, I saw a photo I had never seen before. It was of a heap of dolls. Some were broken, overlapping each other, just like naked mannequins...

GLOSSARY

Aryan: You had to be "tall and blond[illegible] This racial doctrine, invent[illegible] in the nineteenth century [illegible] taken up by Hitler, [illegible]bsolutely no scientific basis. According to the definition, only the populations [illegible] of Northern Europ[illegible] particular the Germans, m[illegible] the "superior elements of humanity."

concentration camp: It's necessary to point out that the first concentration camp was crea[illegible]3. Situated in Dach[illegible] Germany, its first inmates were Hitler's polit[illegible] opponents, as well a[illegible] elements and ho[illegible] who were banned b[illegible] Nazi regime. In 1944, t[illegible]ermans set up 20 concentration camps, and 165 labor camps.

extermination camps: This was [illegible] Auschwitz-Bir[illegible] also Chelmno, Belze[illegible]obibor, Maïdanek and [illegible]blinka. The Jewish populations of Europe were sen[illegible] to these death camps to be gassed.

gas chambers: The latest studies b[illegible]pecialists of the period prove[illegible] that the gas chamber[illegible]ied out on the "menta[illegible]as early as January[illegible] The gas used is ca[illegible]oxide, or Zyklon B. [illegible] Croci shows in this story, the Germans got rid of th[illegible]bodies by burying them in mas[illegible] graves, or burning them in crematoria.

Einsatzgruppen: These special troops[illegible] made up of SS and police, created the first ghettos in Poland and, when the USSR was invaded, proceeded to eliminate Jews and communists.

genocide: This word means the extermination "according to a coord[illegible] and methodical plan[illegible] nation or ethnic group by another.

Holocaust: In the Bible, this term [illegible] "a sacrifice in which t[illegible]hole victim is burned." [illegible]nglish-speaking countrie[illegible] this term to designate [illegible]xtermination of the Jews by the Nazis.

kapo: In the camps, this prisoner, Jew or non-Jew, supervised and directed a group of prisoners.

Sonderkommando: "The special commando." In the story, it says that no one ever comes back alive from the Sonderkommando! Always Jewish, this prisoner was responsible for emptying the gas chambers of the corpses so that they could be incinerated. It is easy to understand why the Germans didn't want to leave any of these witnesses behind them.

Shoah: This Hebrew term has two meanings: "destruction" and "catastrophe." It also means the extermination of the Jews by the Nazis.

the final solution: This was the name given by the Nazis to the secret program whose aim was the partial, then total, extermination of the Jews.

Special Treatment: In German, Sonderbehandlung was the code word the Nazis used to talk about the gassing of Jews.

victims: It is estimated that Nazi barbarism killed over 5 million Jews. This is without counting the massacres of Russian civilians on the Eastern front and the extermination of Gypsies. The Germans were judged for these "crimes against humanity" in the Nuremberg Trials from October 18, 1945 to October 1, 1946. Since then, a "crime against humanity" has become part of international criminal law. The following is an extract of the legal definition: "…the assassination, extermination, enslavement, deportation or any other inhuman act committed against any civilian population, before or during war, or any persecution for political, racial or religious motives."

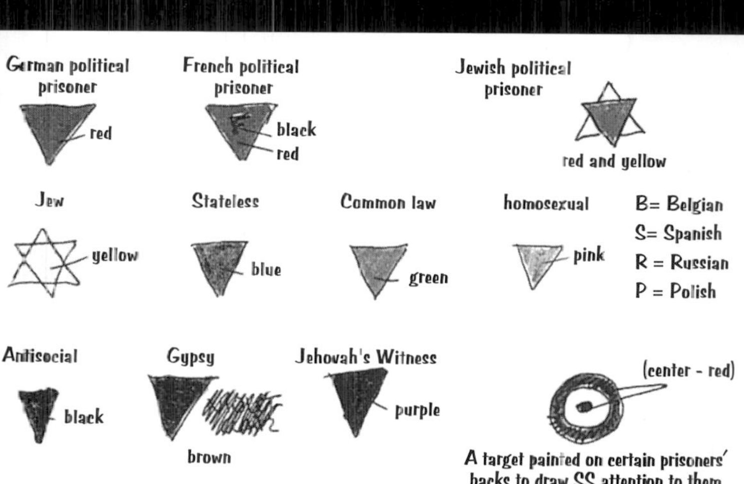

These badges were sewn onto the inmates' uniforms so the Germans could see where they came from. In preparatory notebook for *Auschwitz* by Pascal Croci.

Preparatory sketch

BIBLIOGRAPHY

SOURCES

Stories and eyewitness accounts in the works of Christian Bernadac, such as *Les Mannequins nus* (*The Naked Mannequins*).

L'Album d'Auschwitz (*The Auschwitz Album*) discovered by Lili Meier, concentration camp survivor.

The drawings and paintings of David Olère

Shoah, Documentary film by Claude Lanzmann, 1985; 4 videocassettes by René Chateau Video.

De Nuremberg à Nuremberg (*From Nuremberg to Nuremberg*), documentary film by Frédéric Rossif and Philippe Meyer, 1989, by Montparnasse Video.

Schindler's List, film by Steven Spielberg, 1993.

Special edition of the magazine *L'Histoire*: "Auschwitz, la solution finale" (Auschwitz: The Final Solution), October 1998.

Le Centre de Documentation Juive Contemporaine, (Contemporary Jewish Documentation Center) 17, rue Geoffroy-l'Asnier, 75004, Paris.

Acknowledgments

The author would like to thank the following witnesses, some of whom are members of Friends of Auschwitz, for their precious help.

Kazimierz Kac
Charles and Micheline Baron
Maurice Minkowski
Renée Eskenazi
Henri Wolf
Henri Borlant
Maryvonne Legret-Garet (my first contact for the project)
Maria Ciszewski
Rosey and Yourek Ciszewski
Maryvonne Braunschweig
Jacques Altman
Thérèse Stiland
Moszek Stiland

Library of Congress Cataloging-in-Publication Data

Croci, Pascal.
[Auschwitz. English]
Auschwitz / by Pascal Croci.
p. cm.
Translated from the French.
Includes bibliographical references and index.
ISBN 0-8109-4831-1
1. Auschwitz (Concentration camp)—Comic books, strips, etc. 2.
Holocaust, Jewish (1939–1945)—Comic books, strips, etc. I. Title.

PN6747.C74A9413 2004
741.5'944—dc21
2003013337

Published in 2003 by Harry N. Abrams, Incorporated, New York

Printed and bound in France
10 9 8 7 6 5 4 3 2 1

Harry N. Abrams, Inc.
100 Fifth Avenue
New York, N.Y.10011
www.abramsbooks.com

Abrams is a subsidiary of